TROPICAL
Modernism

TROPICAL
Modernism

by James Grayson Trulove

Title Page: Taylor House, Frank Harmon Architect
James West, Photographer

First published in 2001 by HBI an imprint of
HarperCollins Publishers
10 East 53rd Street
New York, NY 10022-5299

Distributed in the U.S. and Canada by
Watson-Guptill Publications
770 Broadway
New York, NY 10003-9595
Tel: (800) 451-1741
      (732) 363-4511 in NJ, AK, HI
Fax: (732) 363-0338

ISBN: 0-8230-5449-7

Distributed throughout the rest of the world by
HarperCollins International
10 East 53rd Street
New York, NY 10022-5299
Fax: (212) 207-7654

ISBN: 0-06-620931-5

Packaged by:
Grayson Publishing
Suite 505
1700 17th Street NW
Washington, D.C. 20009
Tel: (202) 387-8500
Fax: (202) 387-6160
JTRULOVE@AOL.COM

Printed in Milan, Italy
by Sfera International
First Printing, 2001

1 2 3 4 5 6 7 8 9 /03 02 01

ACKNOWLEDGEMENTS

The author would like to express his appreciation to the architects, designers, and landscape architects for contributing their
work. I also wish to thank Il Kim, Mario Schjetnan, and Richard
Cho for their assistance in identifying projects for inclusion in
this book.

Contents

Foreword   6

Cohen House	Toshiko Mori Architect	8
Teng Residence	SCDA Architects	22
House in Celaya	Grupo LBC/Arquitectos	34
Hogan/Mayo House	Cheng Design	42
1A House	TEN Arquitectos	52
Olabuenaga House	Ettore Sottsas	60
LV House	Rocio Romero	76
Neutra Beach House Addition	Steven Ehrlich Architects	88
Las Lomas House	Grupo LBC/Arquitectos	98
Taylor House	Frank Harmon Architect	108
Coronation Road West	SCDA Architects	124
Ritenour House and Garden	Mia Lehrer + Associates, Mark Mack Architects	132
Palm Beach House	Harry Elson Architect	140
Elizondo House	Gilberto L. Rodriguez Architecture	154
Elizondo Pavilion	Gilberto L. Rodriguez Architecture	164
Sennett Lane	SCDA Architects	174
Scheer House	Hugh Newell Jacobsen Architect	182

FOREWORD

Houses designed and built in tropical and subtropical climates often exemplify the critical ideas of modern architecture advocated, for example, by Le Corbusier and Mies van der Rohe. These ideas include extensive use of glass, decompartmentalized, open floor plans, and the unification of interior and exterior spaces. These modernist houses are often minimalistic in design and are frequently built with local materials. Vibrant colors are often used on the exterior and interior (although stark white is also favored) and the furnishings are typically of modern origin as well.

The houses presented in this book exemplify this modernist esthetic and highlight the work of some of the most creative residential architects working today. Houses such as the Guest House on the Gulf by architect Toshiko Mori and the Neutra Beach House Addition by architect Steven Ehrlich are contemporary reinterpretations of existing modern houses on their respective properties. Mori's project shares its site with a house designed by Paul Rudolph in 1957. Ehrlich's work is an addition to a 1938 house by Richard Neutra, considered a historical masterwork of modernist residential architecture. In both cases, the architects took great pains to relate to the existing houses without appearing to mimic them.

Many of the houses featured in *Tropical Modernism* are sited in locations with spectacular views and lush surroundings, giving the architects an ample opportunity and a perfect excuse to create designs that fully open the residences to the outside.

The extensive use of glass in tropical regions requires that equal attention be given to providing proper shading from the intense sun. Chan Soo Khian of SCDA Architects in Singapore integrates wooden louvers into the design of most of his houses. In the Teng Residence, for example, fixed wooden louvers cover the sheer glass walls which in turn have panels that open to allow for natural ventilation. These louvers not only block the sun but offer privacy as well. Grupo LBC/Arquitectos in Mexico use white louvered aluminum planes to cast cooling shadows over decks and patios.

One of the most remarkable houses presented here is the Taylor House by Frank Harmon Architects. Its design addresses many of the practical concerns one encounters when building in the tropics, from hurricanes to scarcity of water to dealing with insects. Perched above the treetops in the Bahamas, the house features a dramatic roof, shaped like an inverted umbrella which collects rain water that is then transported through a stainless steel pipe to cisterns at the base of the house. To protect against hurricanes, which the house has thus far successfully withstood, it is designed to "zip-up" so that all openings can be sealed against the winds and rain. The major open space, designed for entertaining and for enjoying the spectacular views, is positioned on the top floor, out of range of the mosquitoes in the vegetation below.

While these and the other houses in *Tropical Modernism* offer unique design solutions for their individual sites, they all reflect the influence modern architecture has had on residences in tropical and subtropical regions of the world.

LEFT: *Teng Residence, SCDA Architects.*
PHOTOGRAPHY: *Peter Mealin.*

Cohen House

Toshiko Mori Architect

Photography by Paul Warchol

This guest house shares its site with a house designed by Paul Rudolph in 1957. Located in Florida on the Gulf of Mexico, the guest house is built on the footprint of a structure destroyed by a hurricane. To protect the new house from storm surges and flooding, it is raised seventeen feet above sea level. Sheltered by live oaks, palms, and mangroves, the living quarters of the house are reached by an exterior stainless steel staircase. The stair becomes the "center" of the house connecting the two-story bedroom wing which contains two bedrooms and a living room with the single-story wing that features an additional bedroom, living room, and kitchen and dining areas.

Low-maintenance materials were used for construction including cast-in-place concrete, powder-coated steel, and clear, opaque, and translucent glass.

PREVIOUS PAGES: *Conceived as a T-shape and elevated 17 feet above mean sea level, the house provides commanding views of the Gulf of Mexico.*
LEFT: *Dining area.*
BELOW: *The dense tree canopy provides privacy and shade.*

Site Plan

Axonometric

GULF OF MEXICO

LITTLE SARASOTA BAY

First Floor Plan

Second Floor Plan

West Elevation

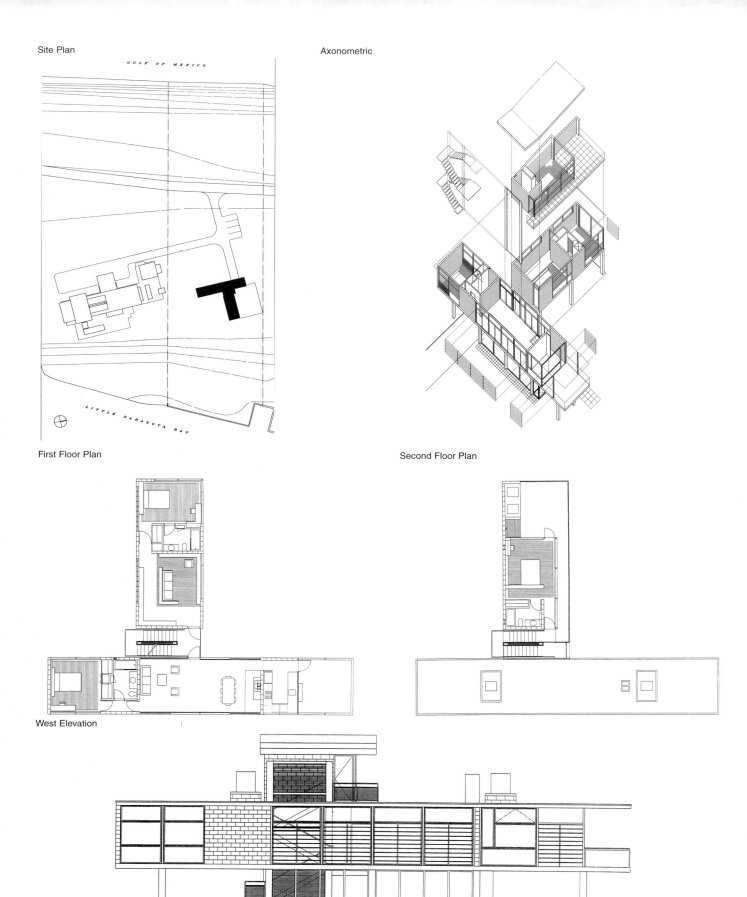

14 Cohen House

E: *Windows are protected from*
s by steel louvers.
OWING PAGES: *Living room in*
tory wing.

ABOVE: *Kitchen.*
RIGHT: *Bedroom with desk designed by the architect.*

RIGHT: *The narrow design of the house along with louvered windows provide excellent cross ventilation throughout the house including the bedrooms.*

Teng Residence

SCDA Architects

Photography: Peter Mealin

Sited on a tight residential lot, this house by Singaporian architect Chan Soo Khian is conceived as a latticed two-story box, constructed entirely of steel and wood and suspended above ground level.

A sheer wall that acts as a visual shield is located a few feet away from the house on the side facing a neighboring lot. Light washes against this wall, brightening the interior of the house.

The façade has a "double skin" consisting of an outer layer of wooden louvers and an inner layer of glass. The louvers are triangular in section allowing a downward view while ensuring privacy. Glass panels open for natural ventilation.

PREVIOUS PAGES: *The patio extends into the first floor of the house.*
LEFT: *View of stairs to second floor from sunken living room.*
BELOW: *Entry.*

First Floor Plan　　Second Floor Plan　　Third Floor Plan　　Roof Plan

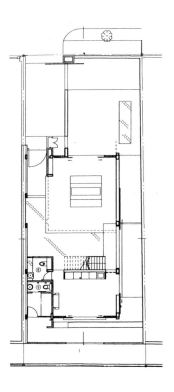
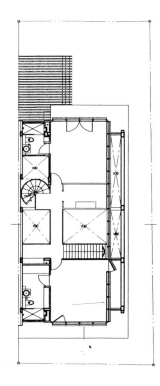
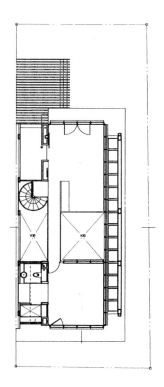
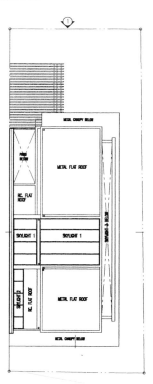

Elevations

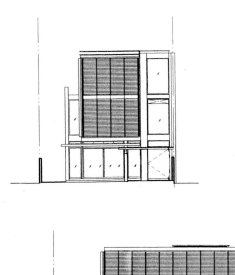
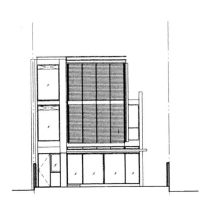

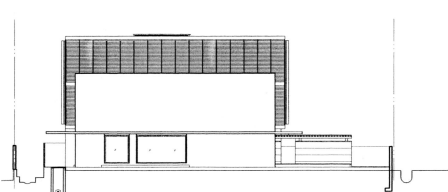

RIGHT: *A spiral stair leads from the second to the third floor.*

ABOVE: *Skylight well.*
RIGHT: *Louvers provide shade and privacy.*
FOLLOWING PAGES: *Kitchen and bedroom.*

28 Teng Residence

House in Celaya

Grupo LBC/Arquitectos

Photography: Fernando Cordero

The design of this weekend house on a Mexican equestrian ranch was inspired by the white fences that divide the pasture grounds. The house overlooks the main jump course. It is divided into two vaulted pavilions joined together by a body of water.

The fence-like design of the house is enhanced by a series of sun protection beams separated from the pavilions and mounted on independent columns. They visually connect the two pavilions and serve as supports for canvas awnings that shade the space where equestrian activities can be watched.

A pond with a wooden connecting bridge separates the living and dining pavilion from the sleeping pavilion.

PREVIOUS PAGES AND BELOW: *The design of the house was inspired by the white fencing that traverses the property.*
LEFT: *Canvas awnings shade the travertine terrace floor.*

Floor Plan

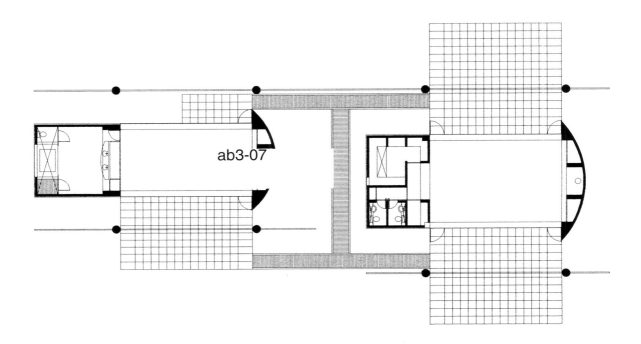

ab3-07

N

Roof Plan

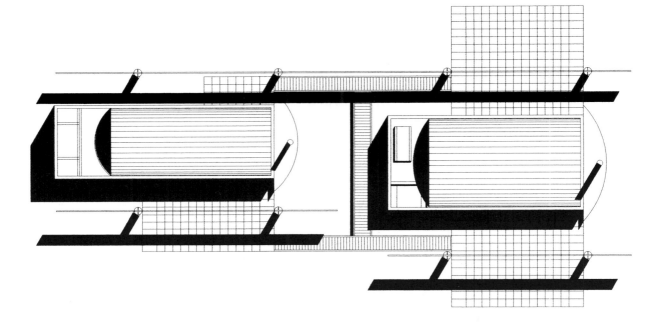

Section

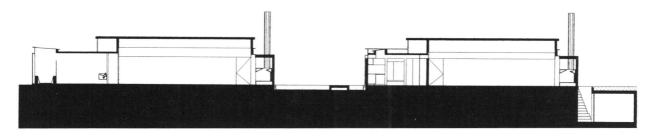

38 House in Celaya

ABOVE: *Detail of wooden bridge and fence-inspired roof beams.*
FOLLOWING PAGES: *Entry façade.*

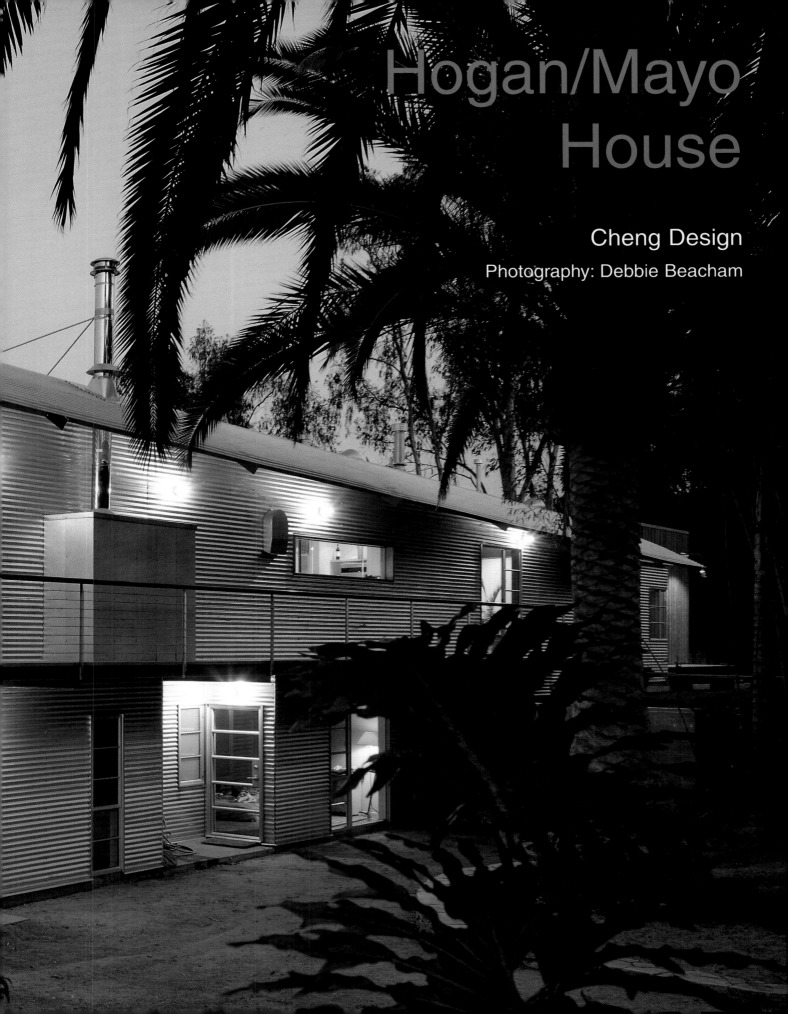

Hogan/Mayo House

Cheng Design

Photography: Debbie Beacham

Wild vegetation including bamboo, palms, and eucalyptus that infused this site in Del Mar, California inspired designer Fu-Tung Cheng to create a house that is at once sleek and modern yet rugged and somehow temporary. "I saw the house as an Airstream trailer or an old Army quonset hut from the Fiji Islands," according to Cheng in an interview in *Architectural Record*.

Using industrial materials commonly associated with modernist architecture such as galvanized siding, steel columns, and concrete, Cheng has fashioned a surprisingly warm and inviting environment. Many of the muted colors, ranging from slate blue to warm ochre, were hand mixed by Cheng who was trained as an artist. These colors are used not only in the plaster walls but in the poured-in-place concrete floors and counter tops as well.

LEFT: *The breezeway leads to a deck and separates the public areas of the house from the private ones.*
BELOW: *Effort was made to preserve existing vegetation.*
PREVIOUS PAGES: *The soft glow of the corrugated metal cladding is in perfect harmony with the lush tropical surroundings.*

ABOVE: *Entrance from the garage via a bluestone walkway.*
LEFT: *The multi-textured exterior includes poured-in-place concrete, wood board and batten, and corrugated metal cladding.*

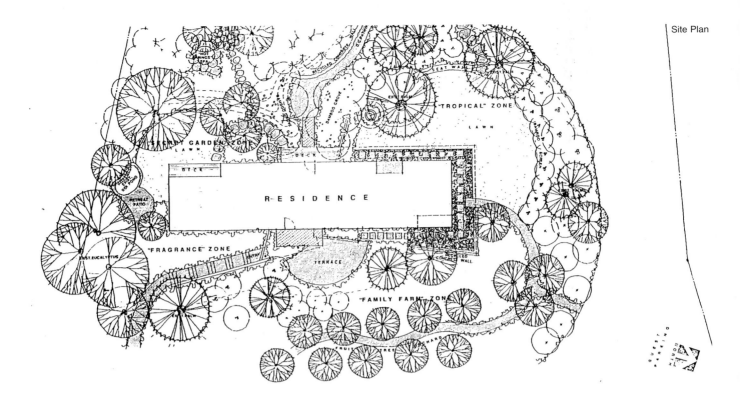

Upper Floor Plan

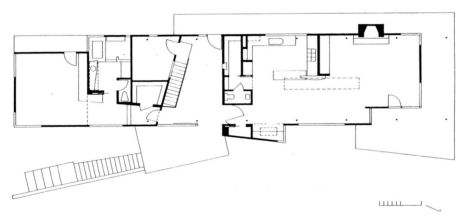

Lower Floor Plan

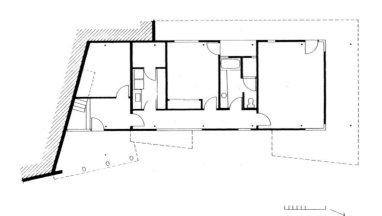

RIGHT: *Found objects such as stones, fossils, computer parts, gears, and other mechanical items are embedded in this concrete stair wall and in other concrete surfaces throughout the house.*

48 Hogan/Mayo House

ABOVE: *Entry.*
RIGHT: *View from the kitchen to the living room. A narrow, long skylight brightens the center of the house.*

50 Hogan/Mayo House

1A House

TEN Arquitectos
Photography: Jaime Navarro

Like a crystal cube, this house appears suspended between the lap pool and the lake at this Mexican resort. Within this glass volume is the living room, dining room, and master bedroom, all separated by a lower, solid volume that contains the service areas. A glass prism is placed over an existing stone basement where two bedrooms are located.

The inclined plane of the wooden roof is supported by thin steel columns allowing it to float over the interior walls. A wooden pergola extends the roof plane over the patio which is an extension of the interior floor, blurring the boundaries between the interior and exterior of the house, a basic tenet of modernism.

PREVIOUS PAGES: *The glass enclosed living room overlooks the lake.*
LEFT: *The inclined roof as seen from the living room.*
BELOW: *A wooden pergola extends the roof plane over the patio.*

LEFT: *View of the lap pool.*
ABOVE: *View of lake from living room*
RIGHT: *View of lake from master bedroom.*

LEFT: *Master bedroom on main level.*
RIGHT: *Light reflecting off the wooden roof emits a warm glow at night.*

Olabuenaga House

Ettore Sottsass

Photography: Undine Pröhl

Best known for his designs for furniture and objects, Ettore Sottsass created this complex and colorful house that synthesizes much of the design vocabulary he developed over many decades. Requiring almost ten years to design and build, the house appears to be as much an object or piece of furniture as it does a dwelling.

Sited high on a hill on the island of Maui, it has commanding views of the coast. The exterior is painted in seven different colors and utilizes an equal number of building materials including stucco, sheet metal, and concrete block. The entire house is organized around a black roof plane resembling a large table supported by black columns. Each colorful box clustered around and under the "table" contains a single room. The entire composition totals 3200 square feet of living space. The interior is equally colorful with much of the furniture designed by Sottsass.

PREVIOUS PAGES: *The playful arrangement of boxes and colors gives the house a child-like quality.*
LEFT: *Living room.*
BELOW: *The house appears as if it were an object placed in the midst of a rugged landscape.*

LEFT: *View of dining terrace and dining room contained in the green box.*

66 Olabuenaga House

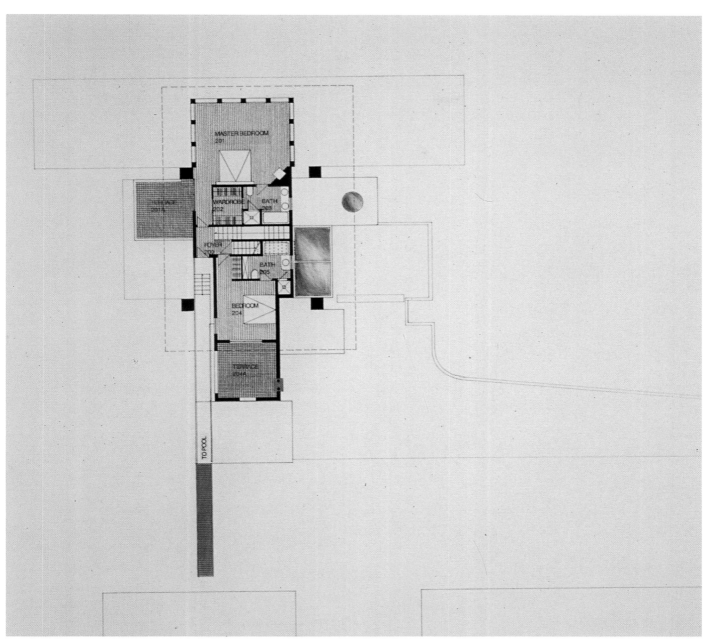

LEFT: *Teak deck with master bedroom suspended above.*

70 Olabuenaga House

LEFT AND ABOVE: *The black box contains storage and separates the living room from the kitchen.*

LEFT: *A collection of old radios adorn the shelves of the gallery.*

74 Olabuenaga House

ABOVE AND LEFT: *Views of master bedroom and bath.*

LV House

Rocio Romero

Photography: Julio Pereira

The LV House is a weekend retreat located on the Pacific coast in Chile. The design goal was to create an inexpensive and compact home that was both functional and low-maintenance. The owners also requested a design that would foster a relaxed, yet elegant atmosphere.

Sited on a bluff overlooking the Pacific Ocean, the home's elongated plan, high ceilings, and continuous sliding doors on the northern façade provide every main room with panoramic views. The two bedrooms, living and dining areas line this side of the house. The bathrooms, kitchen, laundry, and closets are tucked in the back along the southern side of the house.

PREVIOUS PAGES: *The low-maintenance exterior consists of zincalume, aluminum, laminated glass, and concrete.*
LEFT: *Living/dining area.*
BELOW: *The house is sited on a rugged bluff overlooking the Pacific Ocean.*

ABOVE AND FACING PAGE: *The northern façade has sliding doors allowing the entire house to open to the ocean.*

PREVIOUS PAGES: *Modern furniture
completes the house's spare
design.*
ABOVE: *The master bed was
designed by Romero.*

84 LV House

ABOVE: *Stainless steel was used*
extensively in the bathrooms,
kitchen, and laundry.
FOLLOWING PAGES: *View of the*
warmly lit interior at night.

Neutra Beach House
Addition

Steven Ehrlich Architects

Photography: Tom Bonner, John Linden

The original house was designed by Richard Neutra in 1938 and rests at the base of a Santa Monica bluff overlooking the Pacific Ocean. The present owners asked architect Steven Ehrlich to design a 3400-square-foot addition that would complement this important modernist house. The addition consists of an entertainment pavilion and pool, additional parking and servants' and guests' quarters.

While not attempting to mimic the original house, the architect successfully draws upon Neutra's vision of blurring the distinction between the interior and exterior. The addition consists of floor-to-ceiling glass on three sides. When the glass doors are open, the 16-foot-wide pavilion becomes at one with its site and the ocean beyond. At the far end of the pool, a stainless steel gate slides open, aligning the house, pavilion, and pool with the Pacific.

PREVIOUS PAGES: *A view of the original house and the addition at dusk.*
LEFT: *Interior of existing house with view of pool.*
BELOW: *Ariel view of the compound adjacent to the Pacific.*

First Floor Plan

Second Floor Plan

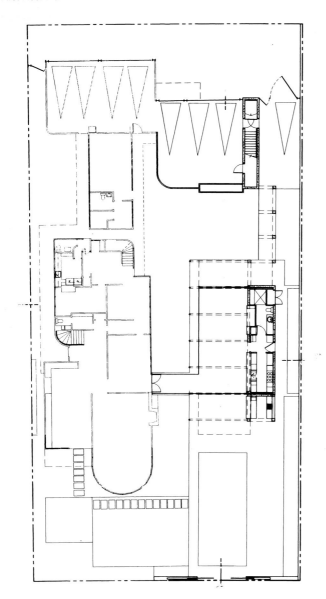

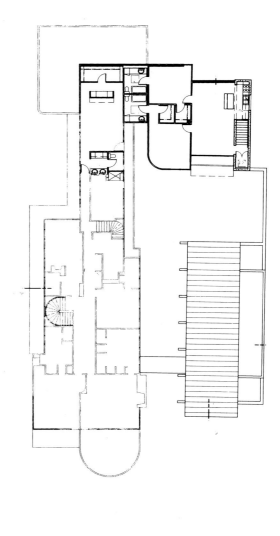

West Elevation

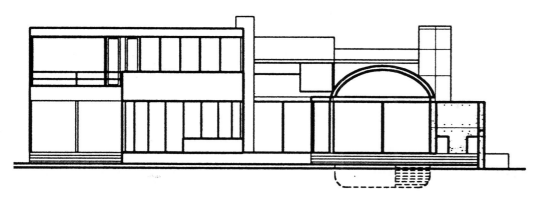

RIGHT: *View of swimming pool with stainless steel gate open, revealing beach and ocean beyond.*

92 Neutra Beach House Addition

94 Neutra Beach House Addition

ABOVE: *Courtyard between existing house and addition.*
LEFT: *Entry and garages from street.*
FOLLOWING PAGES: *View of entertainment pavilion at dusk.*

Las Lomas House

Grupo LBC/Arquitectos

Photography: Fernando Cordero

This L-shaped three-story house in Mexico appears as a monolith from from the busy street on which it is sited. Inside the "L" however, the house becomes quite transparent, embracing the private garden and a large, existing ash tree. Decks overlook the garden from each of three levels. These decks are sheltered by white louvered aluminum planes which cast shadows that appear as fine lines along the south and east façades.

Modulated quarry stone sheaths the north façade and protects the house from dominant winds and street noise. This wall is submerged into a large rectangular pool, which has the effect of lightening its mass.

A library on the third floor has its own boat-shaped terrace and appears to exist independently from the rest of the house, floating alone in the tree tops.

PREVIOUS PAGES: *View of the house from the garden.*
LEFT: *Extensive glazing extends the living room into the garden.*

Ground Floor Plan

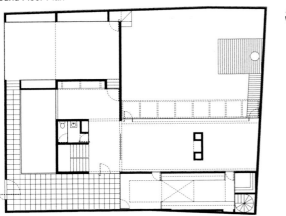

N

RIGHT: *The aluminum lattice work for the decks allows filtered light into the garden.*

First Floor Plan

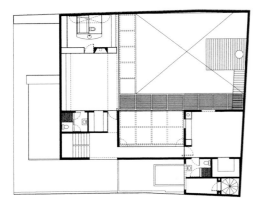

Second Floor Plan

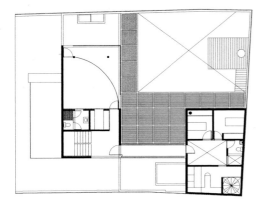

East Elevation

Section

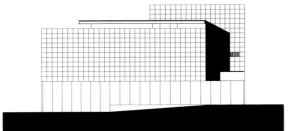

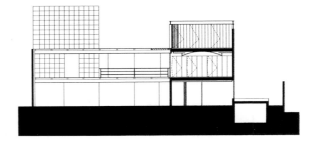

102 Las Lomas House

LEFT: *The north wall rests in a pool of water.*
ABOVE: *The third floor floats among the tree tops.*
FOLLOWING PAGES: *The house turns its back to the busy street.*

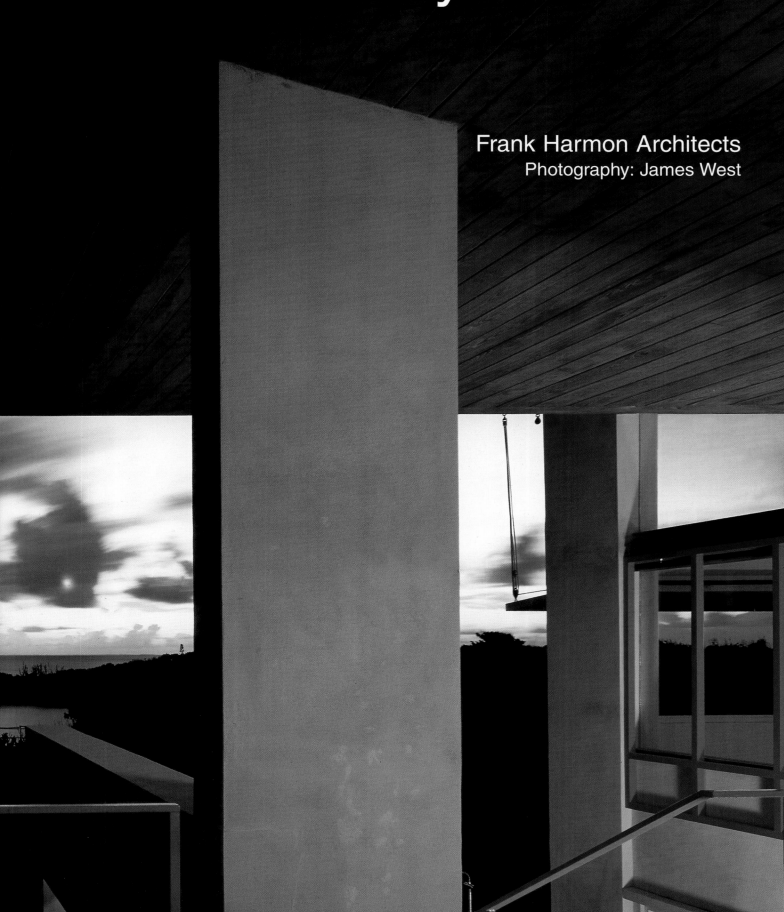

Taylor House

Frank Harmon Architects
Photography: James West

In the Bahamas, residents must get their drinking water from rainwater runoff from the roofs of their houses because there are no wells in the coral reef. To collect this rainwater, architect Frank Harmon designed a roof for this house—located in Scotland Cay, Bahamas—that is like an inverted umbrella with a drain in the center. Rainwater flows down the drain through a steel column into cisterns below.

The Taylor House's design is that of a simple cube sheltered by this big roof that shades the house and creates a venturi effect in an ocean breeze. Because the roof projects the view upward and outward, occupants feel as if they are living in the sky. The living room and kitchen are placed at the highest level, above the trees to catch the breeze and provide occupants with spectacular panoramic views of the ocean, sky, sunsets, and storms. Here they are also out of the range of the mosquitoes in the dense forest below.

To protect against the onslaught of gales and hurricanes that are frequent visitors to the Bahamas, the house was designed to "zip-up" in bad weather. All major openings have sliding doors or shutters.

Towering above the surrounding lush tropical forest, the Taylor House infuses practical solutions into a crisp, modernist design vocabulary.

PREVIOUS PAGES: *From its elevated perch, the house merges with its tropical surroundings.*
LEFT: *The living room and terrace enjoy commanding views of the ocean.*

PREVIOUS PAGES, LEFT, AND ABOVE:
To rise above the trees, the house
was constructed three stories high.

Site Plan

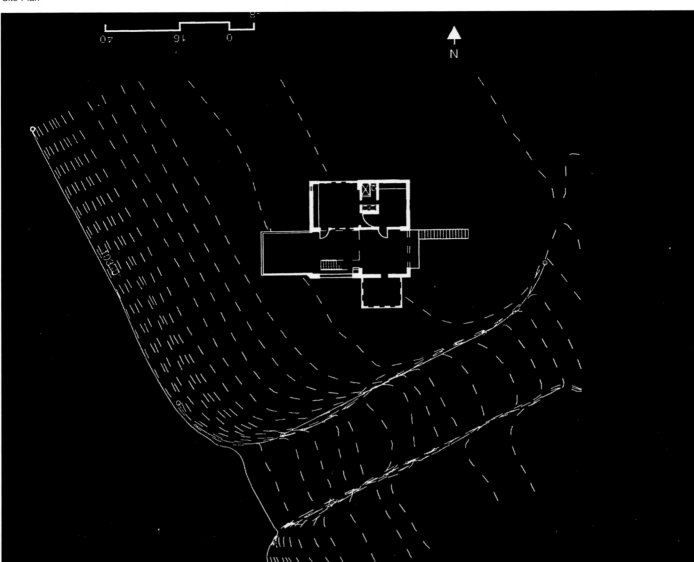

Section

116 Taylor House

Third Floor Plan

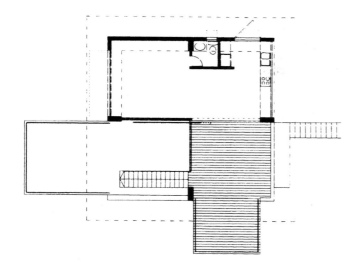

Axonometric

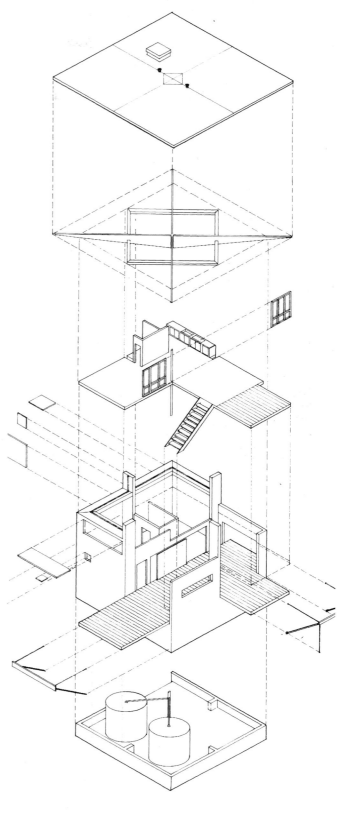

Second Floor Plan

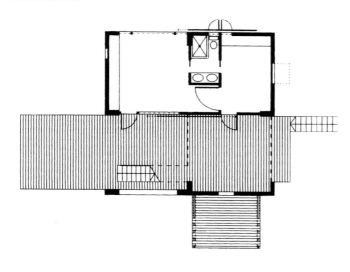

First Floor Plan

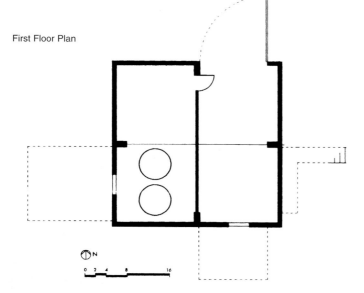

N

0 2 4 8 16

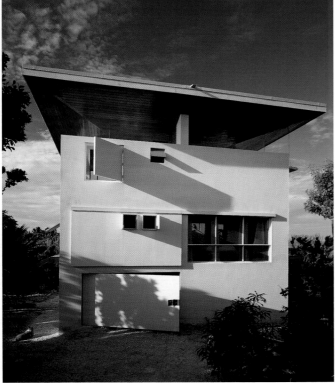

TOP LEFT, LEFT: *The architect designed a system of flaps, shutters, and rolling doors that allow the owners to carefully secure the house during storms.*
RIGHT: *The middle level contains the master bedroom and guest rooms.*

ABOVE AND RIGHT: *The middle level features a balcony and a screened porch for sleeping in the night air.* FOLLOWING PAGES: *Terrace with shower adjacent to master bedroom.*

Coronation Road West

SCDA Architects

Photography: Albert Lim

Overlooking a coconut grove in Singapore, this house transcends the traditional typology of a vernacular tropical house while retaining its essence. Architect Chan Soo Khian uses a modern, minimalist design vocabulary to address the spatial and climatic issues endemic to the tropics. Careful attention was given to integrating the surrounding landscape and pool with the interior.

The house consists essentially of two boxes, one is heavily anchored to the ground while a smaller one, a pavilion, floats over a reinforced concrete wall that connects the two. The east elevation is designed with maximum glazing to take advantage of the view of the coconut grove. A large movable wood screen provides shade and is mechanically controlled to slide across the entire façade. The west elevation has less glazing consisting instead of separate interlocking planes of timber cladding, concrete, and glass. Wooden screens help to diminish the overall scale of this façade.

PREVIOUS PAGES: *West façade with main house and guest pavilion.*
LEFT: *View of living room overlooking swimming pool.*
BELOW: *Screens provide a filter for the harsh tropical sun.*

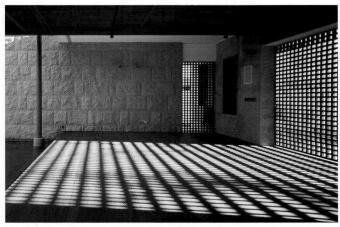

First Floor Plan

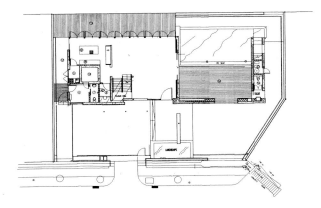

Second Floor Plan

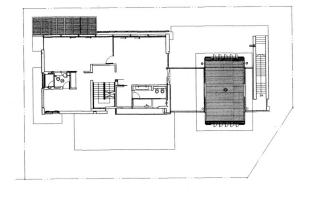

Third Floor Plan

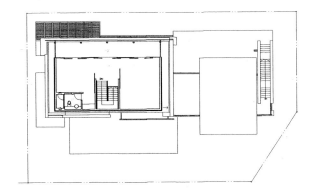

West Elevation

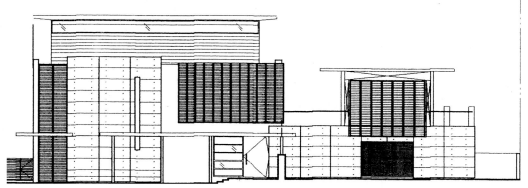

128 Coronation Road West

RIGHT: *Pivoting panels accommodate changing sun positions throughout the day.*

ABOVE AND LEFT: *Through the use of screens and other shading devices, the interior opens seamlessly to the outside.*

Ritenour House and Garden

Mark Mack Architect
Mia Lehrer + Associates Landscape Architect

Photography: Steve Gunther

Great harmony exists between this renovated 6000-square-foot house and its garden, designed for a jazz guitarist and his wife. The house is sited on a three-quarter-acre sloping site in California overlooking the Pacific Ocean.

Inspired by the exterior colors of the house and the Brazilian roots of the client, the planting palette is decidedly tropical. Warm colors appear in bands of lantana, and border penstemon in a raised four-foot-wide planter that extends seventy-five feet. Four groupings of double Mexican fan palms anchor this pool terrace planter at the eastern end. Bougainvillea and nasturtiums speckle the sloped edges to harmonize with the tropical color palette of the gardens.

PREVIOUS PAGES: *Tropical plantings surround the outdoor entertainment terrace.*
LEFT: *Entry.*
BELOW: *Wave-like steps lead from the entertainment terrace to the swimming pool.*

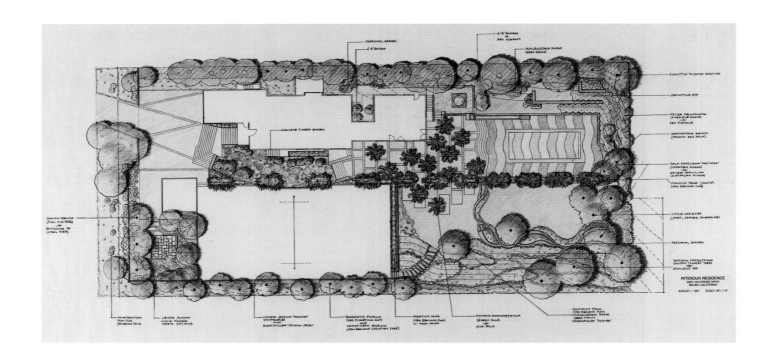

136 Ritenour House and Garden

LEFT: *Paving detail.*
ABOVE: *North elevation of house.*

LEFT: *Outdoor fireplace as viewed from the garden terrace.*
ABOVE: *The entry terrace features turf circles in a field of black Mexican pebbles.*

Palm Beach House

Harry Elson Architect

Photography: Paul Warchol

The program for the remodeling of this Palm Beach, Florida house required transforming an existing 4500-square-foot residence into a contemporary villa, a third again as large with gardens, a pool, and pool house.

A formal axis through the remodeled structure links the public entry court to the private rear garden, terminating at the new pool house. The solid, symmetrical entry façade screens the interior from public view. In contrast, the open asymmetrical garden façade reinforces the relationship between the inside of the house and the outside private garden rooms.

The interior was reorganized and enlarged to create a loft-like public zone flanked by a series of secondary private spaces. A long, covered porch serves as a transitional space between the interior of the house and the rear sunken garden and pool.

PREVIOUS PAGES: *View from the pool to the rear porch.*
LEFT: *Expansive glazing blurs the distinction between interior and exterior spaces.*
BELOW: *Entry.*

Site Plan

Floor Plan

RIGHT: *Garden façade.*

144 Palm Beach House

146 Palm Beach House

ABOVE: *View of pool house from garden façade.*
ABOVE LEFT: *The long, covered porch serves as a transitional space between the interior and exterior of the house.*

LEFT: *The custom dining room chandelier was designed by Donald Lipski.*
RIGHT: *Entrance foyer.*

ABOVE: *Master bathroom.*
LEFT: *The material pallet is spare but warm, creating a subtle background for the owners' eclectic art collection.*
FOLLOWING PAGES: *Rear porch at dusk.*

Elizondo House

Gilberto L. Rodriguez Architecture and Urban Design

Photography: Carlos Tardán

Sited adjacent to a national park in Mexico with dramatic mountain ranges as a distant backdrop, the architects designed this house to both mimic the contours of landscape while retaining its own sculptural form. The low, horizontal structure is punctuated with vertical elements, recalling the peaks of the mountains. The pure, white volumes contrast sharply with the rich blues of the sky and deep greens of the surrounding fauna.

The white stucco walls reflects the hot sun in this region, helping to keep the house cool. Aiding in this task are high ceilings and carefully planned cross ventilation throughout the residence.

The views of the Sierra Madre are exploited in all rooms facing south while an internal patio was created to be enjoyed from the formal and informal dining rooms. It also provides additional light and fresh air to the interior.

PREVIOUS PAGES: *The house unfolds across the landscape.*
LEFT: *Entry.*
BELOW *: Extensive glazing on the south elevation provides dramatic views.*

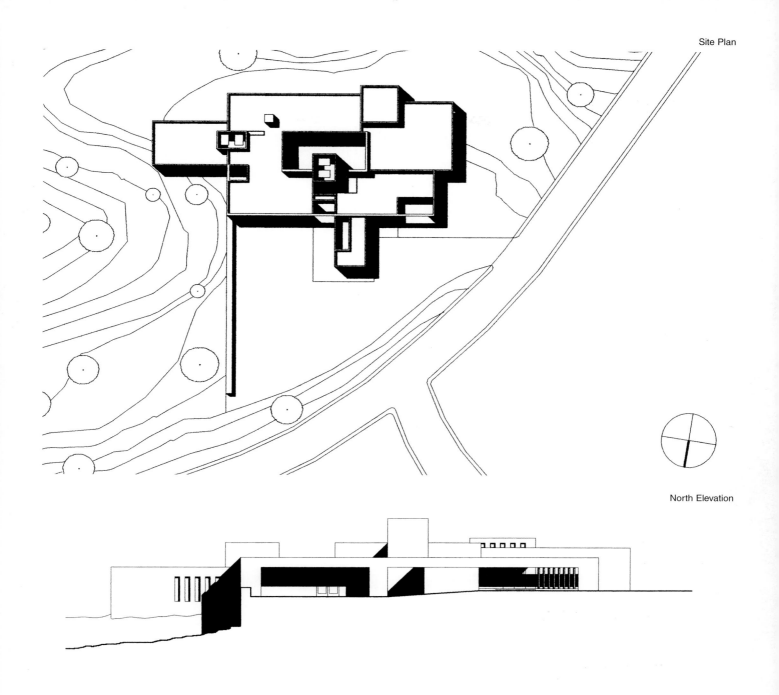

Site Plan

North Elevation

South Elevation

LEFT: *The interior of the house is designed to provide ample cross ventilation.*

LEFT: *View of interior courtyard.*
TOP: *Kitchen.*
ABOVE: *Dining area with view of courtyard.*
FOLLOWING PAGES: *View of south façade at dusk.*

Elizondo Pavilion

Gilberto L. Rodriguez Architecture and Urban Design

Photography: Carlos Tardán, George Taboada

While the addition of this pavilion to the Elizondo house completed the program by adding a pool and an area for entertaining, it also exists as a distinctive piece of architecture.

Because of the difficult, sloping building site, the pavilion was partially buried into the hillside, its roof becoming an extension of the main garden providing a large terrace with panoramic views of the Sierra Madre.

While the designs of the main house and the pavilion are radically different compositionally, continuity is established through the use of common building materials such as white stucco, travertine marble, oak, and river stones.

PREVIOUS PAGES: *View of entry façade and pool.*
LEFT: *Pool as seen from the pavilion.*
BELOW: *View of pool from roof terrace.*

Site Plan

0 5 10

planta de conjunto

First Floor Plan

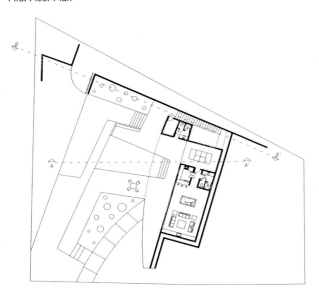

Section

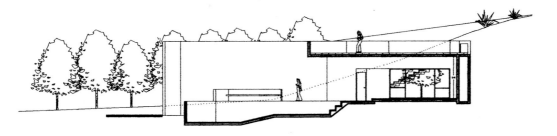

ABOVE: *Mountain views from the terrace.*
RIGHT: *Stairs to roof terrace.*

RIGHT: *Dining area.*

170 Elizondo Pavilion

ABOVE: *View of pavilion with pool.*

172 Elizondo Pavilion

ABOVE: *Original house overlooks pavilion.*

Sennett Lane

SCDA Architects
Photography: Albert Lim

Designing two adjacent houses for a three-generation family was the architect's challenge for this suburban site in Singapore. His solution was to create two facing towers with communal open spaces. These spaces consist of a series of landscaped and paved court-yards including a water courtyard bisect-ed by a walkway. The living room, kitchen, dining room in each tower are adjacent to these outdoor spaces. The second and third floors of the towers consist of bedrooms and bathrooms topped off with roof terraces.

These intricately detailed steel structures use laminated glass to form sky-bridges connecting front and rear bedrooms on the third floor. All external steel is hot-dipped and galvanized to be weather resistant. Extensive use is made of wooden slats for sun-shading screens throughout both towers.

PREVIOUS PAGES: *The east and west façades are organized around a pair of floating cubes of steel, glass, and timber.*
LEFT: *Matching living rooms face each other across the courtyard.*
BELOW: *Entry court.*

First Floor Plan

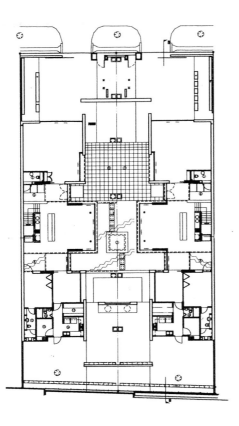

Second Floor Plan

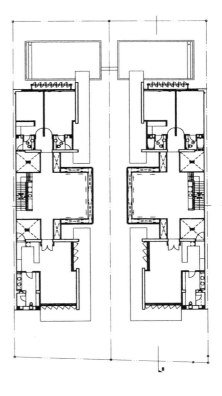

Third Floor Plan

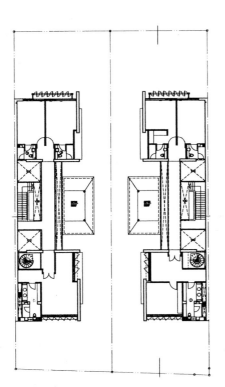

Roof Plan

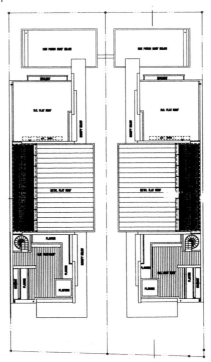

RIGHT: *View of water courtyard.*

178 Sennett Lane

Front Elevation

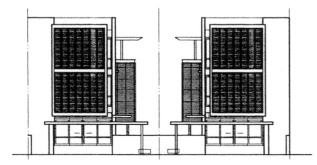

Rear Elevation

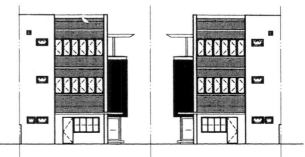

180 Sennett Lane

LEFT: *Wooden screens are used for privacy and shading.*
ABOVE: *View of laminated glass sky-bridge.*

181

Scheer House

Hugh Newell Jacobsen Architect

Photography: Robert Lautman

Strict design codes dictated the street-side appearance of this four bedroom house and guest house located in a planned community in Florida. The living room pavilion however, concealed behind the ten-foot-high wall that surrounds the property, was subject to no such restraints. Here, the architect was free to create a dramatic, glass-sheathed living space that serves as a modernist counterpoint to the surrounding traditional architecture. The living room is connected to the main house by an equally impressive glass corridor.

The entry, pavilion, rectangular swimming pool, and entry to the guest house at the end of the pool are on axis creating a focused view through the length of the property.

Laminated glass is used for the pavilion and corridor to provide security in the event of a hurricane. The glass remains intact if broken by high winds.

PREVIOUS PAGES: *Strict community design codes dictated the street-side design.*
LEFT: *The drama unfolds behind the walls.*
BELOW: *Entry façade.*

ABOVE: *View of living room pavilion
from the guest house (right).*
FOLLOWING PAGES: *View from the
living room pavilion toward the
guest house at the end of the pool.*

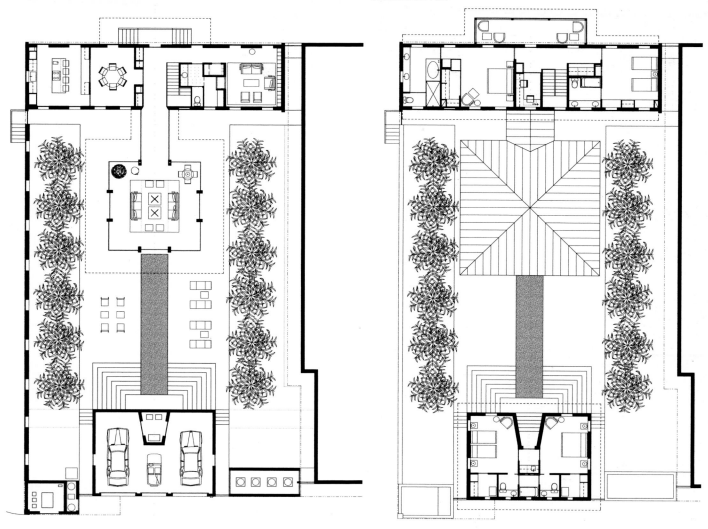

LEFT: *Library in main house.*
ABOVE: *Dining room with view of kitchen in main house.*
ABOVE RIGHT: *Bathroom.*
FOLLOWING PAGES: *View of the living pavilion from the guest house at night.*